creepy creatures

CONTENTS

Published by Creative Paperbacks
P.O. Box 227, Mankato, Minnesota 56002
Creative Paperbacks is an imprint of
The Creative Company
www.thecreativecompany.us

Design and production by Ellen Huber
Art direction by Rita Marshall
Printed in the United States of America

Photographs by 123rf (Adrian Hillman), Alamy
(Stefan Sollfors), Bigstock (Yuriy Chaban), Dreamstime
(Rolf Aasa, Ciuciumama, MorganOliver, Sielan,
Viktorfischer), iStockphoto (Antagain, Evgeniy
Ayupov, Michael Braun, Chris Downie, Eric Isselée,
TommyIX), Shutterstock (David Good, Ingvald
Kaldhussater, Sebastian Kaulitzki, D. Kucharski &
K. Kucharska, Henrik Larsson, wacpan, Monika
Wisniewska), SuperStock (Minden Pictures, NHPA),
Veer (klikk), Wikipedia (André Karwath)

Library of Congress Cataloging-in-Publication Data
Bodden, Valerie.
Ticks / by Valerie Bodden.
p. cm. — (Creepy creatures)
Summary: A basic introduction to ticks, examining
where they live, how they grow, what they eat, and
the unique traits that help to define them, such as
their ability to swell with blood.
Includes bibliographical references and index.
ISBN 978-1-60818-234-3 (hardcover)
ISBN 978-0-89812-797-3 (pbk)
1. Ticks—Juvenile literature. I. Title.
QL458.15.P37B63 2013
595.4'29—dc23   2011050287

First Edition
9 8 7 6 5 4 3 2 1

ticks

VALERIE BODDEN

You are walking in the woods on a summer day. Suddenly, you see a brown dot on your arm. You look closer.

It is a tick!

Dog, or wood, ticks are some of the most common ticks

Ticks are **arachnids** (*uh-RAK-nidz*). They have two body parts and eight legs. Some ticks have a hard covering over their bodies. These are called hard ticks. Soft ticks do not have a hard covering over their bodies. But their skin is tough and leathery.

Arachnids do not have feelers called antennae (*an-TEH-nee*) on their heads

Wood ticks (left) are very small—about 3/16 inch (.5 cm) long

Most ticks are brown or black. Some ticks are red or yellow. The smallest ticks are about the size of a sesame seed. The biggest ticks can be almost as big as your little toe.

A tick can attach itself to human skin and feed on blood for many days

This tick is feeding on a cat

There are about 825 kinds of ticks. Bat ticks are soft ticks found on bats. American dog ticks are hard ticks. They like to grab on to dogs, deer, and even people.

Hard ticks look like flat seeds when they are not full of food

African birds called oxpeckers, or tickbirds, eat ticks

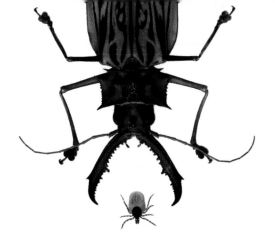

Ticks live around the world. Most ticks live in fields and woods. Ticks have to watch out for **predators**. Birds, beetles, and spiders all eat ticks.

Ticks cannot fly or jump, but they can crawl

Ticks are **parasites**. They bite people and animals. Then they eat their blood. A tick sits on a branch or weed and sticks out its front legs. When an animal passes by, the tick grabs on to it.

The castor bean, or sheep, tick latches on to sheep and cattle

About a month after the eggs are laid, tick larvae are born

Female ticks lay eggs.
Tick babies are called **larvae**.
The larvae look like small
adult ticks. But they have
only six legs. After feeding
on blood, the larvae **molt**.
They become young ticks
called nymphs (*NIMFS*).
Nymphs have eight legs.
Nymphs eat a lot and molt
one or more times. Then they
become adults. Most ticks
live one to three years.

Ticks' bodies swell, or get fat, when they eat. Soft ticks can weigh 10 times more after they eat than they did before. Some hard ticks can weigh 600 times more after eating!

Some fully fed ticks can be the size of a pencil eraser or larger

A full tick will drop off an animal and onto a plant

Nymphs climb up plants to look for their next meal

Some ticks can make people and animals sick. To stay safe from ticks, people should wear long sleeves and pants when they are in the woods or tall grass. As long as ticks are not on you, it can be fun to see these blood-sucking creepy creatures up-close!

MAKE A TICK

You can use a balloon to make a tick that swells. First, cut out eight long, thin paper rectangles. These will be your tick's legs. Fold each leg back and forth several times, like a paper fan. Tape four legs to each side of the balloon after you have a grown-up help you fill the balloon. You can fill it with air or with water. Watch how it swells, just like a tick!

GLOSSARY

arachnids: small, eight-legged animals like spiders and ticks

larvae: the form some insects and animals take when they hatch from eggs, before changing into their adult form

molt: to lose a shell or layer of skin and grow a new, larger one

parasites: plants or animals that live on or in other plants or animals and take food from them

predators: animals that kill and eat other animals

READ MORE

Fredericks, Anthony D. *On One Flower: Butterflies, Ticks and a Few More Icks*. Nevada City, Calif.: Dawn Publications, 2006.

Hirschmann, Kris. *Ticks*. San Diego: KidHaven Press, 2004.

WEB SITES

Entomology Image Gallery
http://www.ent.iastate.edu/imagegal/ticks/
Click on the links to see tick pictures and videos.

Pestworld for Kids: Ticks
http://www.pestworldforkids.org/ticks.html
Learn more about deer ticks and the problems they cause.

INDEX